60 Odd Years

NANCY DUPUIS
The Writer in Me

Order this book online at www.trafford.com
or email orders@trafford.com

Most Trafford titles are also available at major online book retailers.

Print information available on the last page.

ISBN: 978-1-6987-1322-9 (sc)
ISBN: 978-1-6987-1324-3 (hc)
ISBN: 978-1-6987-1323-6 (e)

Library of Congress Control Number: 2022919745

Trafford rev. 11/03/2022

 www.trafford.com

North America & international
toll-free: 844-688-6899 (USA & Canada)
fax: 812 355 4082

Contents

Preface

"As I headed out to share a meal with old friends here on the Island on that Boxing Day, I was reminded of the many lasting friendships we, as a family have made over the years as well as the new ones I continue to make as I go about my daily life now. I believe human contact is a necessity in each and every one of our lives. We crave acceptance and love, as humans. Where we find it, is mostly up to us."

Chapter 1

My Childhood Years

Where to begin? Recollections of a little girl (4 years old) at her Grandmother's wake at the house next door in the country – a coffin in the dining room; 1956, a time when this was still a common occurrence; I now understand as an adult the value of holding wakes as family and community come together to pay their final respects to the deceased. Our Mom always took us (or dragged us along as I used to call it) to wakes and funerals from the time we were small children. I get that now and actually am appreciative. I now pull on my "good" clothes and attend these sombre occasions out of respect as well. Even last evening, as I attended yet another wake, I was surprised at the sheer magnitude my attendance meant to a brother of the deceased. He, an old family friend and who was mourning the loss of his sister, mentioned two of our brothers had been in during the afternoon visitation, and now here we were, the two sisters. Our Mother and Father, especially in later years, had been such good friends with this family, all living in the same village. A brief chat with another member of this family made me realize how important attending that wake really was as she spoke of her late husband's visits to the retirement home where our Mother had lived for a time, and he'd always come home telling her what Janetta had been knitting today. That very comment warmed my heart so, as I conjured up a picture in my mind, of my Mom, knitting needles click-clacking away, enjoying news from outside the four walls of the facility she now called home.

But, back to life in that old white house in a small country village (Appleton, Ontario). I was the oldest; a girl, five other children to follow soon after. There was no running water, no indoor toilet, and just an old wood stove that my Mother used to cook her heart out on. The winters were cold and the beds were brought downstairs each winter as it was much too cold to sleep upstairs with the windows frosted over. Between the wood stove in the kitchen and an oil burner in the hallway separating the living room and dining room, we were at least kept half warm in the winters. I vaguely remember four bedrooms upstairs – my Mother and Father's room, two other bedrooms where each of the four boys shared a room with another and then a room where I slept, later on sharing that room with a crib in which my little sister slept. I remember a story my Mother used to tell me of the first night that baby came to sleep in my room. The first cry in the night, and my Mother came to the baby, only to find me up trying to soothe the little girl. I apparently had thought the baby was my responsibility now that she slept in my room.

As I start to write this story, I think back to my Grandparents home, next door to ours. It was the fall of 1956 and my Grandmother had just died and was laid out at home, a normal thing to do in those times. I was just 4 years old at the time and I can still see a vision of that coffin along one wall of what I believe used to be the dining room off the kitchen. There was a Victrola machine for playing music in the entrance way to the house on the corner, the dining room to the left. To the right of the entrance was the little parlour where my Grandmother had lain in bed 12 years prior to her death, bedridden with arthritis. We have an old photograph of my Grandfather sitting with her beside her bed. He looked so very tired, but was with her to the end.

The upstairs to the house was out of bounds, as no real need to go up there. I can still remember the upstairs though as I must have taken a look or two up there as a youngster, being inquisitive and wanting to know just what was up above when no one was looking. A cousin recently confirmed that they had visited when she was just a child and staying overnight, she remembered the upstairs was indeed very, very cold in the winter months.

The home of my grandparents in Appleton, Ontario

These were the times of no running water, wringer washers, frozen laundry hanging about in the winter taking its due time to dry, outhouses – a time when my Mom and her sister-in-law shared the same maternity dress for their monthly visits to the family doctor. We were not rich, but we were blessed by what we did have and the generous neighbours who all contributed to each other's well-being in times of need.

My Grandfather lived in that house for a number of years after my Grandmother's death, before moving to a rooming house in a nearby town, in later years. During the day, he continued to travel out to help at the farm one of his sons had taken over from him earlier on in life and did that for as long as he could. I can still remember the old truck, blue it was, I think. In the evenings, he could be heard playing the fiddle for hours on end. He enjoyed playing the fiddle well into his late eighties and usually performed at the local Fair's annual fiddle contest. I can remember our whole family sitting on the old grandstand, on a Saturday night, feeling so proud that this was our father, father-in-law, and most of all, just Grandpa.

Grandpa had a phone, we didn't. My Mom would make the trek across the back field if she needed to make a call. I remember gooseberry bushes and red currant bushes in Grandpa's yard, that my Mom and I would pick, and then she would put away for the winter the many bottles of jam from these seemingly just berries growing on a bush - so delicious later spread on homemade tea biscuits, again made by my Mom's loving hands.

As more brothers & a sister appeared at our house next door, a huge garden was needed to keep everyone fed. I still remember many a spring day when we kids would sit on the hill at the back of the house watching my Grandfather with horse and plough work the land for Mom and Dad. The most prevalent of crops in that garden was white navy beans. Bushels and bushels of beans would be stored in the cold cellar for the winter months ahead. There were many days in the winter months we'd come home from school at lunch time to enjoy a big bowl of steaming, hot bean soup much like the pea soup of our day now. To dress it up just a bit, my Mom would throw in a can of tomato soup for a little variety, and also, I suspect to make it go just a little further.

I remember fondly of a time I was vacationing on the farm for a week with my cousins and we were heading into the big city to shop. A first for me, and I think

Grandpa knew, as he stuffed a $2 bill into my hand. I never forgot that. I couldn't have been more than 8 or 9 years old at the time. I often think back now to that morning and wonder what Grandpa would think of how times have changed since those days. In later years, I travelled twice a day back and forth to and from the city like it was just part of the normal routine, during my working career.

My Grandfather was a tall, lanky man, very quiet, but oh so well read. He always subscribed to a number of newspapers right up until the time of his death in 1980, at the age of 96. Apparently he ate bacon and eggs every morning, although I can still recall the odd corn flakes box in the kitchen at the old house next door.

As I think of my Grandfather now that I am an adult and living in a world so very different from his, I think fondly of who he was, bringing into this world 7 children, each making a mark on life in their later years in their own way. Grandchildren arrived, Great-grandchildren too and the descendants continue to this day. The family tree is strong, something of which he'd be oh so very proud of – I see him as I type this, standing unassuming with pipe in hand. This was just pure simplicity in the enjoyment of his pipe and how he lived. A life well lived, born 18 March 1884, the youngest of 12 children, he passed away on February 29, 1980. My own son had been born just a few short months prior to Grandpa's passing. Mom in her quiet way, reflected that the world was only so big, and some had to move on to make room for the new ones. I will remember her saying that to me that day always and the impact that sentence had on me. Thought provoking it was! My Mother's words still resonate with me today, at that time though helping me to surrender to the mystery of death, a little piece at a time.

In those days, school started when you were officially six years of age; no kindergarten in those times. Because my birthday fell in February, it meant that I couldn't begin school until I was almost 6 ½ years old. One of my brothers was born on the second day of January; you guessed it – no school till the next fall. So, my Mother had a little black chalkboard on the kitchen wall and it was there I learned to print the alphabet and numbers to 100 before I started school.

I remember being so shy, the thought of going to school was daunting! When visitors came, I'd sit at the top of the steps going upstairs and listen until they had left. Mom could never understand in later years how I could be given such responsibilities with some of my work in the federal government as a Special Events Coordinator and travelling on my own - having to actually talk to people and come back to the office again having to provide my recommendations, with great detail and clarity. She still saw me as the shy little girl, not the adult or I suppose the person I'd now grown into.

School was a red brick two-room building, located almost across the road from our house. One room (known as the little room) housed Grades 1-4 and the other room (known as the big room) held the senior classes, Grade 5-8. Grade 1 proved as mortifying as expected, witnessing one day a student just a year or two older than me getting the strap, obviously for some wrong doing. Mortifying as well is a memory of being left to take the brunt of a broken glass on a school window caused by a snowball. I hadn't been quick enough to run away, the only one left standing there when the teacher came to see who had been the cause.

My Mother and Father were caretakers in those days at the school, and one day my Father let me go with him to the school as he cleaned and scrubbed the floors. I received my first and only actual spanking ever after I was caught snooping through some of the desks. Just some inquisitiveness on my part, but my Dad saw it as perhaps reason to lose his job (this part-time job adding much needed income to a large family like ours) but more importantly he wanted me to know that what I had done was wrong. From that day forward I held my Father in high esteem. I was deeply embarrassed that I had disappointed him and vowed never to let that happen again.

In the early primary years, I developed a love of spelling. I was always the winner of the school spelling bees, or at least close to the top. I recall a time I came home from the two-room school across the road, in tears. I was sure my Mother would be so upset with me; I'd only achieved a mark of 99% in spelling that day. Fast forward to 2018 and that school reunion held the long weekend in August – there was a spelling bee, a cursive writing contest and a printing contest amongst other things. I, as part of the organizing committee of that little two room public school reunion, couldn't wait to be one of the participants in the spelling bee. What fun that was – no, not the top place winner, but darn close!

I recall box lunches signifying Valentine's Day at the school, where the boys would bid on the girl's beautifully prepared lunch in highly decorated cardboard boxes (usually an old shoe box), with the funds raised then being sent to the Red Cross, I believe. My Mother would always ensure there would be heart-shaped shortbread cookies in my boxed lunch, lovingly cut out with her metal cookie cutters and iced with pink homemade icing (that pink icing likely coming from mixing a bit of cherry juice from a jar of cherries to make it ever so pretty).

We didn't have much growing up, but we always had enough – we never went to bed hungry. Our Mother, a farmer's daughter had learned to cook and bake at a very young age. I can't remember a day without a home-made dessert on the table for at least two of the three meals. I still miss her home-made buns and pies. One afternoon, an inquisitive little girl pushed a chair over to the pantry cupboard, crawled up and stood upon it to reach the butterscotch pie cooling on the second shelf. With one little finger poised to dip into that meringue, the expectations were more than she bargained for. Down came the pie, crashing all over – the meringue, the yummy filling, the flaky crust everywhere – all over the little girl, all over the floor, with the mother's good glass pie pan laying broken on the floor. No matter, another pie was quickly whipped up before the evening dinner, with me receiving a good scolding, I'm sure.

I remember visitors to our home and visiting with others in the community, especially on Sunday afternoons or evenings. My Mother attended Ladies Aid meetings, me in tow with her usual contribution to the fellowship time after the meeting – fancy rolled pinwheels sandwiches (cream cheese with a cherry in the centre of each sandwich, cream cheese drizzled with the cherry juice from the bottle).

From the time I was a little girl, comfort food types of meals were always on the table. Creamy mashed potatoes with a good helping of sliced carrots all from the garden, slathered in butter and a good roast of beef and gravy - the traditional Sunday evening supper fare. And, not to forget - always a dessert. My mother had come from the farm and was well versed in cooking for a large crowd. Homemade pies and buns were her specialty and, she was well known for these two, all visiting hoping that she might have made a bit extra, to allow for seconds. I still think of my brothers in later years all snitching a homemade bun from the basket prior to large family gatherings. Mom's buns and apple pies will always remain as a memory of my Mother, forever.

Walks to and from the village to mail letters for my Mom or to pick up something at the grocery store, provided an adventure of sorts. Bottles in the ditches along the side of the road; easy pickings to be turned in once you arrived at the store for a penny or two cent candy. One day, I got a little mischievous using the money sent with me for a stamp at the post office to mail a letter for my Mother, to buy some penny candy instead.

I often think back to that day and wonder what I did with that letter or who it was meant for.

Halloween during my childhood was so very different than what it is today. Everyone knew everyone so it was great fun to dress up; even the adults would try to fool neighbours as to their identity. My Mom would spend days making homemade fudge as the treat to be had at our house. Most of the village children headed straight for one house in particular in the village. The old fellow would sit in his chair in the living room holding court and insist that we sing, dance, or recite a poem prior to receiving a treat (usually a shiny new dime) which was seen to be a large sum of money to a little country bumpkin like me. I always think of these times when I hear the phrase "trick or treat" now in later years.

I attended that little two-room school from Grade 1-6. Arbour Day - the morning was spent cleaning up the school, windows, and all and, picking up whatever trash had accumulated over the winter months outside. Then after lunch, the dreaded ball game. I didn't like sports and I sure didn't like playing ball. Vague memories of a game called Red Rover, Red Rover are formulating in my head, as I write this as well. My school wardrobe consisted mostly of hand-me down dresses, (new to me) brought from Hamilton, Ontario by a favourite Aunt and Uncle. They had one daughter just a little older than the cousins up the road and I. My cousins out in the country as well as I, looked forward to these visits after which we would break open the boxes and attempt a try at dressing up, feeling very posh indeed. I do remember though a trip to Ottawa one year when I was about 12 years old coming home with two brand-new dresses, and a new spring hat for church. I was ecstatic! I think that was the first time I'd ever had a new dress, let alone two new dresses! One was pink candy-striped; I can still picture that cute little dress with its dusty rose sash around the middle. The other was a blue floral; memories etched in my mind forever.

I believe it was in one of these last years at school in Appleton, that I remember my Grandfather coming across the road from his house on the corner to the school, quite distraught with the news that one of his young grandchildren had been killed in a farming accident that morning. My Aunt had visited just the day before and I had held this little two-year old playing as such, unaware of the terrible fatality to come. My Aunt was most likely on her way to town for her monthly pregnancy appointment clothed in one of the maternity outfits she and my mother shared, my Mom babysitting, thus the memory of me cuddling this little child, my cousin. Attending this wake and funeral with my Mother and Father, I remember seeing first hand the experience of loss; the mourners stopping to shake hands with the fellow (a hired hand) who had accidentally run over the child, spoke mounds to me even as a child of the closeness of community. A little girl was born to my Aunt and Uncle shortly after this tragic accident. Ironically, this little girl died suddenly at approximately 10 years of age from the likely cause being pneumonia. Their graves now side by side, a little brother and sister who had never known each other.

Our family moved to Balderson, Ontario for a year when I was in the 6th grade at the Appleton school. Arrangements were made with neighbours to allow me to finish my school year at Appleton. I would stay at a neighbouring farm during the school week and go home to Balderson on weekends. A teacher who lived in a nearby village would drop me home on Friday nights or my Dad would pick me up on his way home from his construction job in the city and then drop me off at the farm again early Monday morning.

Balderson, Ontario – memories of that year include Grade 7 at a new school, this particular grade consisting of me and 7 boys in again a country schoolhouse. Puberty, boys; the shyness remained. A visit to the cheese factory next door each Sunday after church for a huge hunk of cheese followed by a lunch of homemade soup, bread and cheese remain forever in my mind. It was the simple comfort food prepared by my Mom that kept us nurtured over the years. Many of these meals enjoyed as a child became part of the staple meals of our own growing family in later life. Small village country life there included an old fashioned telephone on the wall, in which your incoming call was likely identified by something like 2 or 3 rings, one long, maybe two short. Listening in on the party line for us kids became a favourite pastime. Mom was not impressed.

The following year brought another change to my teenage years, a move to Richmond, Ontario. My Dad had found the drive from Balderson to Ottawa and back each day, just a bit too much. Richmond brought new opportunities for him later on when he bought a couple of dump trucks and hit the road, usually with one of my younger brothers now old enough to drive one of them.

Grade 8 was not one of my favourable times, nor were my high school years. There had never been a lot of focus at home on what each of us might choose as a so-called career later on in life; we were just to get a basic education and make our way into the work world in order to provide for ourselves in a future life, something I sure didn't think much about in Grade 8. I did however take a part-time job at a local restaurant after school and on weekends as soon as I could. I was developing a more independent streak, and hadn't liked the answer given by my Mother, when I asked for a pair of white Nancy Sinatra style "go-go" boots. Between my work at the restaurant and numerous babysitting jobs, I was indeed able to get those boots and wore them proudly, much to the envy apparently of some, something of which I wasn't aware of until years later in a light-hearted conversation with some old classmates.

High School, again not a favourite time in my life – my parents had enrolled me in the 5 year academic program, but after one year of that, I and they had figured out that I would be better off in the 4 year business program offered. So onto a new program in school (typing, bookkeeping along with the usual English, Mathematics, History) – I now started on my awareness of the administrative side of things; although unknown to me at the time, this was something that would bode well in my future.

When I think back to my childhood, I realize how painfully shy I was, but always aimed to do my best at school, always striving for the best marks possible. The teen years were painful; I was shy, gangly, backwoods it seemed where I came from. I felt inferior to some of the others both in public and high school as I felt I came from a family of have-nots. I now realize I had so much more than others.

I continued to work at the little restaurant in Richmond, enabling me to purchase the new school clothes I myself chose each fall, unaware of in all likelihood of the huge help I was providing financially to my parents, with a large family still at hand to feed and clothe as well. I remember in earlier years being taken by Mom and Dad to pick out school clothes at the LaSalle store in Bells Corners and our clothes would be put on lay-away until final payment was made, usually just before the new school year. This tradition carried on for years.

A visit from an Insurance man, actually my Mom's cousin shortly after my graduation and the start of my first job in Ottawa, still to this day leaves me with a chuckle. I had started work in Ottawa right after finishing my Grade 12 year (a payroll clerk in a fuel oil/construction company). Mom and that insurance salesman had likely discussed my new job and a bit of the future Mom likely had in mind for me and she had probably thought it time for me to invest some of that money earned; (my salary at that very first job was actually $50/week back in the seventies.) The insurance man trying his best to entice me to invest, assured me that this would be a good thing to do as my future he was certain would include a husband and then children. I was adamant that there would be no husband, and certainly no children, ever. Fast forward a few months later, married! And the years to follow, children! Hmmmmm!

Six months or so later while working at that first job, I received news from a Federal government office that I was to come in for a typing test – (during our final year of our business course, it had been suggested that we apply for federal government clerical positions in nearby Ottawa). Success!

A new job; a clerk in the Library and Archives Canada building on Wellington Street in the city – wow; in six short months, I had doubled my salary (now $100/week). It was here that I was invited to go on a blind date; a friend's boyfriend and she were going out, he didn't have a car but his friend did, thus, I became the blind date to that friend. It was an office Halloween party - I still remember my costume (a devil all dressed in red and black – hmmmm, some of you say, a little bit mischievious back in those days too;)

The rest is history, as they say! The next day a Sunday afternoon drive, the four of us; two weeks later I asked him to marry me! And yes, he said "yes" neither of us knowing at the time that this union would last another 34 years until his death separated us in 2006.

Chapter 2

The Military Years

Marriage – August 05, 1972; after meeting Ray in the fall of 1971 (myself 19, Ray 21) we were married the following summer, a whirlwind romance I guess some would call it. We moved into row housing on the base at Uplands in Ottawa, Ontario and thus the beginnings of our married life. I always felt from the moment I met Ray that I wanted to be part of this couple thing forever. I guess our forever was the 34 years of marriage we were so fortunate to have together. I had always thought that we would be together for so much longer, maybe even till we were 104, what with all the good drugs now available. I think back often of how we were robbed of our retirement years and those plans we had made together. The plan had been to buy a truck and 5th wheel, and off into the sunset we would go, camping all over the United States in the winter and then coming back into Canada for the summer months to spend time with the children and grandchildren. For a long time after he passed away, I remember seeing trucks and 5th wheels on the highway and I would almost throw up, my emotions getting the better of me. It took a long time for those feelings to pass. One could now say, although not the travel Ray and I had planned, I am sort of doing that great explore all on my own now across Canada.

Times were lean those first few years in the military; we managed though. We were blessed over and over so many times with friendships made at every new posting. Second hand cars, military housing, working hard, having fun and raising our family was the norm.

Our oldest daughter, Lisa arrived in the spring of 1973 while we were still living on the base in Ottawa.

I stopped work when Lisa was born; I wanted to take care of her, myself. I dressed her in the cutest little dresses, all of which had to be ironed just perfectly after a wash and dry outside on the clothesline. The baby was born in the spring so enjoyed all her naps that summer outside in the pram at the back door. What a peaceful time that was. My Mom and Dad were close by in Richmond, so spent many hours visiting with their first grandchild. Dad was always so good with little kids and he loved them so, so much that my Mom hardly ever got a chance to have "just her" time with the new baby. So, we had Mom come in for the day and see what would happen – it took until late afternoon when Lisa finally backed up towards Grandma, with a pick me up on your knee please kind of nudge, warming up to her ever so slightly. Mom was thrilled.

In 1974, we were off on our first posting away from Ottawa and my family. Canadian Forces Station Lowther was a little radar station in northern Ontario, west of Kapuskasing on the road west towards Hearst. We lived in a trailer, (a three-bedroom mobile home) another new experience. The community was tight knit as there were only about 30 trailers on the Station. Some members and their families lived in town (Kapuskasing) those members making the trek in and out by military bus each day. Everyone got to know each other quickly and lifelong friendships were forged. Our second daughter, Jennifer was born here in July of 1975. I recall a number of false alarms with her impending arrival. It was likely nerves just knowing that we were quite a way from the hospital. I do recall one of those trips, having a flat tire about 10 minutes from the hospital in Kapuskasing. Oh, my nerves! Finally she arrived, although 10 days after her due date. A full head of long, thick, black hair; so different from her sister who was so fair.

I remember one morning in the hospital, the nurse brought her in for me to feed and cuddle and took one look at me and whisked her away. She apparently thought she belonged to some other mother. No, she's mine and I wouldn't trade her for anything. It took us a few days to name her as we'd thought for sure she was a boy all along. But then, Jennifer she became!

Every two weeks on a Saturday, we would make the trek to town (Kapuskasing) for groceries and staples. It was a day out for me. The funniest memory of those trips for groceries was in the winter, when we'd remove Jennifer's hat and snowsuit and people would stop to stare at her hair. Whatever was forgotten on the list on grocery day was either borrowed from a neighbour or done without until the next shopping trip.

There was no work to be had on the Station for me, so we engaged in the process to foster a child from the area. A few months later, Jennifer was 8 months old, Lisa probably about 2 ½, our foster child arrived – a little girl from northern Ontario, 10 months old. Things got busy. This wee one stayed with us until our posting to Petawawa, Ontario, the following year. Foster children had to remain in their home region.

Bears were a regular occurrence on the Station, as were black flies! Every day, sometimes twice a day, all windows were closed for the trucks coming by spraying for black flies. Bears were plentiful and a quite common scene. I remember a neighbour cooking a nice ham one afternoon for supper, and a bear came to visit, apparently sniffing the simmering supper smells from the fan over the stove vented to the outdoors.

1976 saw us posted to Canadian Forces Base Petawawa, Ontario. This was closer to home for me (only about two hours away) and an area of the province I was fairly familiar with. Petawawa being a hard core army base, Ray was gone a lot. Army manoeuvres occurred on a regular basis. I spent my time babysitting for neighbours when they needed a spot for their children to come for lunch or before and after school. Ray was posted to Cyprus in the fall of 1978, leaving me alone for the first time in my life. This was a 6 month posting so would carry over the Christmas season into the spring. I had finally went for my driver's licence before he had left;

I'd been putting it off but no more! No being stranded for me. We had just purchased our first new vehicle prior to his leaving for Cyprus, a Ford Zephyr station wagon. That vehicle served us well in the years to come.

I had a conversation recently with an old friend from our days at Canadian Forces Base Uplands (Ottawa, Ontario). While Ray was away in Cyprus in 1978/1979, she was home visiting her family in Burnstown, Ontario while her husband was also away on a navy vessel somewhere out in the deep seas, far from home. So, we got together for a weekend. What fun was had in that house in Burnstown. But then, a snowstorm on the Sunday I was to go home. Nothing doing, I was determined to make it home because parents were depending on me to babysit the next morning in Petawawa. So, her Dad followed me up the back road to make sure I made it to the highway at least. Later on apparently, he told his daughter, I sure had guts starting out on a stormy day like that. I laughed when I heard that as I must have had that stubborn streak way back then too.

Yes, that was and still is just me! Invincible! And maybe incorrigible too?

It was shortly after Ray's departure for Cyprus, I realized our family was about to grow. When news reached Cyprus, Ray's colleagues threw him a little party, complete with a "Congratulations" cake with a baby's soother on it. I have the photo still. 1978/79 was a time before all the social media as we know it now. My only contact with him over that 6 month period was a ten minute phone call once a month, or letters which took forever it seemed to go through the military mail service. I recall the lists by the phone awaiting those once a month calls and never having enough time to get through the list.

Returning home just prior to our son Michael's birth in the early spring of that year (1979), Ray had a little mishap on the bus in from Ottawa to Petawawa, Ontario – dropped his kit, scattered all over the bus, had to be collected and put together before leaving the bus. Everyone getting off the bus, but no Ray? I thought he'd missed the bus, but then there he was – a sight for sore eyes.

It was here that we found our love of camping as a young family – a hardtop tent trailer, then a second larger one in later years; we had found something we could afford to do as a young family. This activity lasted well over 15 years. Campfires, marshmallows, breakfast cooked outside on the Coleman – all wonderful memories of those years.

Our next posting (1981) was to Canadian Forces Station Baldy Hughes in the interior of British Columbia. The Station being out in the bush country, we chose to set up house in Prince George. Ray would take the military bus back and forth to the Station each day, while I dropped off the children at the nearby babysitter and headed to my job, an equal distance but the other direction to the north of the city. I had obtained employment here as a mailroom clerk and fill in receptionist for the pulp and paper company, Northwood Pulp and Timber in their corporate offices adjacent to the mill. The road going in was not so fun – steep embankments (not sure of the rate of survival if you ever went over the sides – no guardrails), with runaway lane signs frequent for the logging trucks.

We were so lucky to be not far from Quesnel, British Columbia where my Mom's sister, Beatrice and her family lived. Bea and Leonard had left Ontario at a young age, Len to work on the railroad. We got to know my aunt and uncle as well as their family while at this posting, with frequent visits to Quesnel, our one and only link to family, being so far away from home. Our son, Michael was only a little guy and he used to call Aunt Bea "Grandma" as to him she reminded him of the Grandma he had left not so long ago in Ontario. Sisters, they must have had an uncanny resemblance to him.

While in British Columbia, we missed things back home; there was no extra money for travel back to Ontario, but we were fortunate enough to make a few camping trips around southern BC during the summer months. Ray was away a bit on courses here as well as manoeuvres – this was a common occurrence in our life in the Forces. I remember one particular instance; he was off somewhere in Ontario and I was holding the fort. "Mom, the hamster's not moving" – (Great, yup, it's dead!) Leaving it in it's cage overnight just in case it might come back to life, kept one little concerned girl (Jennifer) happy. But, the next morning the truth had to be told. What to do? In true Nancy fashion, I picked up the whole cage, hamster and all and threw it in a green garbage bag. After all it was winter, no burials taking place this week. Eventually the little ones settled down, and then … heading out to work about a week later, kids in the car on our way to the babysitter, backing out of driveway, this cute little blonde boy in his car seat about 2-3 years old spits out "Say goodbye to Hammy Hamster, Jen!" Yes, it was garbage day!

We were blessed to have visitors from home always when away on postings, our posting to British Columbia no different. My Mom and Dad always managed to scrape together enough dollars to make a visit, wherever we were posted. We were always so happy to see them and show them the place we now called home. It was an education for all. Ray's Mom and Dad also visited from the southern Ontario area and they too got to see the many different places we were posted to over our years with the military.

Next up, posting (1985) to Headquarters, Ottawa, Ontario; was great, close to home again, family nearby. It was here Ray completed his Grade 12, something he'd been meaning to do for a long time. We were all so proud of him – the kids certainly understood the effort he was putting in as they were now in the middle years of school so got it that Dad was working hard at work during the day at his regular job and then school at night. No pain, no gain, was the lesson learned.

It was here we also decided to purchase a home out in Russell, east of Ottawa. The kids were so excited, there was a swimming pool. Only thing was they had to wait till we got home from work to go swimming if they arrived first after school. I can still hear the complaints – "you can't even swim, Mom! Why do we have to wait for you to come home?"

Our time in Russell was short-lived. Before we had made that big purchase, Ray had asked if there was any sight of a posting in the future – no, they said! Six months later the news came, (1990) we were off to Canadian Forces Base Calgary, Alberta. It was sad to have to sell the house but also came the excitement of a move, yet once again. The kids were not so thrilled, again having to leave the school and friends they were just getting to know.

Calgary, it turned out was short-lived as well. We weren't all that happy living in a city, although we were on the Base. We didn't seem to make friends as easily here as we had other smaller spots, although our oldest met the love of her life while in Calgary and many years later actually still lives there. Meanwhile, Ray had been on the watch for other employment and decided to take his retirement. He applied on a job posting with the Prince Edward Island Reserve Regiment in Charlottetown, Prince Edward Island so off we went in January 1991, driving across Canada and bits of the United States, on a bit of a winter road trip. Lisa stayed behind with friends to finish her semester in high school and would join us later that winter to finish that year in the Maritimes. As I look back on that decision now, probably not one of the best ones we had ever made. She would've been fine staying in Calgary. She was mature beyond her years for a 17-year-old.

The Island – very small to the kids who had recently been used to big city living; memories float back of Lisa's first car (I think Dad had bought it for her in the hopes she would stay and not return to the West) – and a loose muffler; Jen learning to drive the minivan (she could hardly see over the dash); Michael loving the snow days (no school due to weather and road conditions) and there were lots of them, and raising havoc on the school bus, always embarrassing his sisters whenever the chance.

Charlottetown, Prince Edward Island to Ottawa, Ontario over and over again and again; my Dad's long illness with both lung cancer and heart disease saw us racing for the ferry once too often. We'd usually leave right after work, drive all night to Ottawa, never knowing what we would find when we got there. Endless trips it seemed but done out of sheer love. Soon the Confederation Bridge would be built connecting the Island to the mainland, a time while we were still on the Island and able to see this massive work in progress and the outcome. I remember the first time we drove over the bridge – Wow! No more racing to catch the ferry!

From our time in Petawawa, Ontario I had always worked either for the Federal Government or a few times for private firms. Every time there was a new posting, it meant a change in the workplace for me as well. I think back of the many friendships we made travelling back and forth across this country. Charlottetown was no different, a transfer once again with the Federal Government, and again, the making of life-long friends.

It was here in Charlottetown that Ray was sent on manoeuvres to the Magdalen Islands for a few days and the pictures he took while there camped on the beach were stunning. A visit here is certainly on my list in the next few years as I continue to explore.

4-H was a big part of our life on the Island, Michael buying a horse for himself and, finding a stable to board her before telling Dad & I. I think he was about 13 or 14 at the time. She was a young racehorse that wasn't fast enough for the track, so between Ray and Michael, they trained her to show in 4-H classes. She remained with us until we left the Island, being sold at that time to a young girl also in 4-H from the eastern side of the Island.

It was in 4-H as a club leader and eventually as part of the provincial team that I learned my capacity for organizing events. There was a national conference coming up in the next couple of years so myself and another stepped up to the plate taking on the co-chairing of organizing this event. This was big – all provinces took part in this annual hosting and it would be Prince Edward Island's turn soon. So, the planning began! We two were working full time at our regular jobs so had to manage the organization outside of our working hours. Job well done! It was so much fun, eventually meeting people from all across Canada (members of other 4-H groups as well as those representing the Royal Agricultural Winter Fair, the Canadian National Exhibition, the Calgary Stampede and the Pacific National Exhibition to name a few). I had no idea at the time what impact the having a hand in organizing this event would have on my life in the next few years - a short time after our arrival in Ottawa in 1998, I became the Special Events Coordinator for the international work in progress at that time for the Canada Revenue Agency, a job I loved; travelling, planning the logistics for conferences large and small, meeting people from around the world.

Michael joined the Reserve Force during our time in Prince Edward Island. He went from a teenager with very long hair to a smart looking young man in a uniform. His Dad sure took a lot of teasing when he showed up with that long hair at the Reserve Unit in Charlottetown that evening 20 some years ago.

It was a time of visiting local craft shops on a regular basis, still do actually. The Island relies on its tourist traffic expecially during the summer months. There is beautiful pottery made here, as well as many other quality home-made crafts. And, musn't forget the yummy preserves; - my favourite being mustard pickles.

Oh, the red clay – sand between my toes; there are so many beautiful and picturesque beaches on Prince Edward Island. I still love nothing better than a walk on the beach, gazing out over the water thinking about what might be beyond its horizon.

Soon it would be time to leave the Island – Ray had left the Reserves for a short stint with a company in New Brunswick, then he moved on to the Canada Revenue Agency (Summerside Tax Centre) in Prince Edward Island.

Jennifer left for Calgary to see what the wild west would hold in store for her. It had been good for her sister and I guess she felt the timing good to strike out on a new adventure for herself. So, she landed in on Lisa for a bit, only to have her boyfriend of the time in Prince Edward Island follow her a short time later to join her in the West, and again as they say the rest is history.

Ray had been asked to take a short term assignment with the Canada Revenue Agency in Ottawa, Ontario in 1998, then asked to come back later that fall on a permanent basis. The timing was good – my Father was not well, and Mom needed our being closer to help out. Although she never would have asked us to move back, I do know she was quite relieved to have us back in the area. Transfers for Ray and myself with our government positions, Jennifer and Lisa now settled in the West, Michael just graduating high school and deciding at the last minute to come with us back to Ottawa also – new beginnings!

We landed in Ottawa in the fall of 1998 and were able to have two more years with my Dad, till his passing in 2000. He loved our visits and we loved being there in their apartment in Stittsville, a stone's throw from Carleton Place (we'd bought a home there shortly after arriving in Ottawa). My Mom and Dad lived on the ground floor and enjoyed being able to see all the comings and goings of the building they now called home. Dad until he was no longer able shovelled the walkway to the main doors faithfully and Mom became a valued member of the group meeting every afternoon and evening in the common room for tea and fellowship, and of course with the organizing of events at the building, she was always at the helm.

Michael joined the military shortly after arriving in Ontario but, unfortunately was injured during Basic training and subsequently left the military a few years later.

Chapter 3

With Life Comes Death

My Dad died in 2000 and Ray in 2006, with Ray's brother Emile also passing away a few years after Ray's death. I will always be grateful that we moved to Carleton Place, Ontario when we did and got established in the neighbourhood and church and re-established with members in the area of my Mother's family. It so helped me with the transition of what was to come.

Ray was an avid fisherman and badminton player. On weekends he was the greatest – always sharing in the household chores and intent at spending time together. In later years, Friday night became our night to kick back and order take-out to enjoy with a bottle of wine in front of a good movie. I so missed that after his passing.

The little beagle dog and the two cats went as well after living good long lives, leaving a great emptiness in the house on our return from work each day.

After his sudden death in 2006 from a cancerous brain tumour, it didn't take me long to realize that I couldn't continue to work and travel as my job required and still maintain that house with its yard work as well. So sold it I did, moving into a condo in the same town. This now afforded me safe haven as well as peace of mind when travelling with work.

Michael and his young family (a little one with them only two weeks old at the time) came back to Carleton Place in 2007 upon his release from the military and were my saving grace so to speak.

Trips south and abroad were taken in the next few years, with friends and co-workers. Cuba, Mexico, and Europe - all places I'd never been before. The Mayan ruins, the turquoise waters of the Caribbean, Vimy Ridge all are forever etched in my mind – great memories of these trips. I did enjoy travelling abroad, however now I want to see Canada, in all its splendour. What a great country we live in and so different from province to province. There are so many places in my own country, I have yet to explore.

Retiring from the Federal government in 2012, I took on a local Fair Board Secretary position to keep up my skills and to give me something to do with my spare time. There, old friends and new formed the welcoming and warm quilt so to speak as I learned all about the compilation of Fair prize books, etc.

Later on that same year though, I had a hankering from something new, some sort of new adventure.

I didn't realize it at the time, but I could no longer live this way; pulled into others drama on a continuing basis, certainly not who or what they thought I should now be. I was the only one that could "fix" me after my husband's sudden passing. I knew I had to do something. The sudden death and all the trappings that came after that, the funeral, selling of the house, what to keep, continuing to work and not really allowing my grief to surface, was taking its toll. Everyone thought I was fine, that I was handling everything with such strength. Only I knew the real truth.

After a brief conversation with my elderly Mom, I decided to pack the car and take off for sights unknown. I had retired; I had quickly realized I had way too much time on my hands, so in the summer of 2012 I researched Kijiji Halifax and quickly spotted a place to rent (furnished) in the area that spoke to me. No need to look any further. I flew down on an overnight trip, met with the people who owned the place and quickly rented it for the next few months. Back home, I had another conversation with my confidante, my Mom. She got it, she understood the depths of my despair and my screeching need to try something different to ease my soul, I suppose. I told everyone I was just going on a little vacation, but I really had no intention of coming back. (Best little "vacation" I ever took!)

So, after putting most things in storage and packing only what I thought I needed for the winter months into the car, I set off for the East Coast early one fall morning with great anticipation as well as a bit of fear. I passed by the village my Mom lived in with a little sigh of "Thanks Mom for believing in me"; I had said my goodbyes the day before. I only went as far as Quebec City that day; that decision had been pre-planned. I had never driven this far before on my own and I wasn't sure of the toll it would take on me. Simple things like filling the car with gas on these long trips had always been done by my husband. I had always been the passenger on those trips of yesteryear.

I headed for a beautiful old hotel, the Chateau Frontenac in the old part of the city right downtown, where my lodgings for the night awaited. I parked the car, checked in and had lots of time that afternoon for a walkabout in the old city, taking in the many sights, and then enjoyed a lovely dinner and glass of wine on an outside patio, a few blocks from the hotel. It was a beautiful fall that late October day, and the leaves were stunning as was the warmth of that day, allowing me to sit outside on that patio and just enjoy the moment, people watching all the while.

I remember the next morning the hotel valet service wanting to help me put my laptop and bags into the car – "No, no need" I quickly said, as I surveyed the trunk and back seat knowing that only I knew the spot those two things had come out of and where they would fit again for the rest of the trip.

The rest of the trip was uneventful, stopping in the Moncton, New Brunswick area the next night, then arriving at my destination the following afternoon. I had set the GPS wrong and somewhere around Halifax I took a wrong turn delaying my arrival by a couple of hours. I was so tired that after a quick pick up of a bit of groceries and unpack of the car, I slept straight through for twelve solid hours. I was so exhausted from not knowing if I could drive this far by myself and also I had sort of scared myself the day before as I realized the impact of my decision. This new place, unknown to me and chosen as I wanted a fresh start with no memories, was indeed going to be home to me for a bit at least until I had a better handle on my health and well-being. I had to make this work.

I knew no one, but was aware of this part of the province as I had once accompanied a group of international visitors with my work to the Peggy's Cove area many years ago, just down the road from my new locale, Glen Margaret, Nova Scotia.

Peggy's Cove, Nova Scotia

The next morning, I was poking around outside checking the yard and outbuilding when up the lane walked a woman from the neighbourhood, bottle of homemade marmalade in hand, to welcome me. I was so touched.

I had noticed a little white United Church up the road within walking distance when I had been down renting the house earlier in the summer, so the first Sunday there I decided to walk up and open the door, hoping for the best. Lo and behold, the woman who welcomed me at the door that morning was the woman from the Bed & Breakfast where I had stayed while checking out accommodations in the summer. In I went and was made to feel most welcome. That Sunday at that little church now over 200 years old was Fellowship Sunday, meaning we all went after church to the little hall next door and enjoyed each other's company as well as some great food, be it sandwiches, cakes, cookies, etc. I will never forget the kindness of one of the men of the congregation who got up from his chair, came across the room, shook my hand and welcomed me to the community. Many from this congregation became such good friends, lasting friendships I must say as I have just come back from a visit to this community once again and am always made so welcome, one of their own.

I didn't realize the true value of what had just happened until a few years later. The friendships made in the Glen Margaret and Hackett's Cove area of Nova Scotia will stay with me the rest of my life. The impact was sincere. Landing in a little community called Glen

Margaret at first in Nova Scotia (NS) and then a few months later in an adjoining community, Hackett's Cove, NS – warm and welcoming people, music and fun times and, oh yes, the tea biscuits and oat cakes – need I say more?

Hackett's Cove, Nova Scotia

Activities were many – to name just a few; Pub night at the Sou'wester at Peggy's Cove, fundraising dinners at the church, house parties in the Cove, the most memorable though being the writing and self-publishing of my first book "Begin Again" in 2015, an intimate story about unsurmountable grief and the power in following your own heart.

It was here I was asked by the local Minister at the little United Church where I was a member, to write down my thoughts as to why I had made such a dramatic change in my life; so, I started to scribble.

- excerpt from "Begin Again" by the Writer in Me (self-published in 2015 with Trafford Publishing)

"Sometimes I think my late husband is watching over me in many ways, like somewhat of a guardian angel and knows and sees what is happening in my life – the good and the bad. When I see the hummingbirds at the feeder, I am reminded of how much he loved those little birds and all of nature – of the quiet, gentle, non-assuming man he was."

I think back often to the many friendships made here over the 4 short years I was in Nova Scotia and I am overwhelmed by the genuine kindnesses shown me – they took me in as one of their own, no questions asked.

I remained in Nova Scotia from the fall of 2012 until January of 2016. A trip back to Ontario in the summer of 2015 had made me realize it was time to go home. I was privileged to spend the last year of my Mom's life with her and will never regret my decision to go home. Having family and friends in the area helped provide a buffer for me when the days ahead got really bad.

-excerpt from a second book, "Where is Home?" by Nancy Dupuis, The Writer in Me (the sequel to "Begin Again", self-published in the late spring of 2019 again with Trafford Publishing)

"I arrived at the ferry terminal a little early that afternoon and took a walk about enjoying the sun. I immediately noticed a number of other passengers waiting for the ferry and who were walking about much as I was, although these were mostly couples. I felt a jealous twinge there and then that afternoon, thinking back to how my late husband and I had never enjoyed those retirement years we had so been counting on. The ferry arrived and all of a sudden I found myself driving onto the ferry down in the bottom floor of the boat. All of a sudden, I was petrified! I was driving down but I couldn't see where I was going; ah, at last the bottom level of the boat. Shaken, I parked the car and found my way to the cafeteria for some food and beverage. I sat there realizing my mood change of the afternoon, saddened. I'd never driven onto a ferry before, let alone down into the jowels of that monstrocity; Ray had always done it. I think back how vulnerable I was that afternoon. Maybe I was just tired from the sheer length of the road trip, realizing how far I'd come from home in the last couple of months or maybe it was because I wasn't quite sure of what the future would hold, now that I'd started on this latest adventure."

These books and a third one titled "In Search of an Old Clay Road" (self-published the summer of 2022 with Trafford Publishing) and now this one; my life story slated for release this fall (2022) have always been my "go to" almost every day – there is so much release in putting my thoughts to paper.

My Mom passed softly away; (March 14, 2017) - below follows the eulogy given by her oldest granddaughter, Lisa during her funeral service.

My Tribute to my Grandma, written in part by my Mom, Nancy, compiled from conversations with family and friends as well as excerpts from writings by Janetta, herself:

Let me start with a writing Grandma had done a number of years ago reflecting on her life:

I was born in Huntley Township on March 07, 1923. It seems like only yesterday that I was a little girl playing in the farm yard with my 2 sisters and 4 brothers. My father farmed 100 acres of land plus another 100 on the adjoining farm where he was raised. Times were hard but everyone was in the same boat. We wore hand me down clothes and others that Mother made for us. We slept on straw mattresses with the straw being changed once a year. We were covered at night with hand-made quilts. Sheets and pillowcases were made from bleached flour and sugar bags. All the men's socks were knit by my Mother. In the spring of the year you helped care for the lambs and the calves. We always had a pet lamb which would follow us into the house. My mother raised turkeys each year, also chickens. I did not like gathering the eggs from under the hens on the nest. All of our bread and buns were baked at home, myself baking both by the time I was 16. The oldest boys helped on the farm or that of a neighbour. In the fall of each year, the threshing mill would pull in to the yard – 1 ½

days for white grain and ½ day for buckwheat. We would
have about 15 men to feed. The table was set with white linen
and the best dishes brought out. Big roast pans of fresh ham,
and another with baked beans, homemade pies and preserves –
everything was grown on the farm. We had an apple orchard
on our second farm and a huge garden and a long row of
rhubarb, also plum and chokecherry trees. I am sure my mother
never bought a jar of jam in her whole life.

Before we went to school it was our job to set the table for
the noon meal. In the winter the men cut wood and again the
neighbours arrived to help saw the wood. Then us kids had to
pile the wood in neat rows to dry out for the following year.
We cooked on the wood stove and heated flat irons on the stove
to do the ironing. We had a cream separator and churned our
own butter. Our mail came to a box about ½ a mile down the
road delivered by horse and buggy in the summer and sleigh in
the winter. It was my job every day to go get the mail.

One paper I remember was the Family Herald and of
course the Almonte Gazette. On Sundays we went to church
and Sunday school in the village and us girls belonged to the
mission band. Later we joined Junior Farmers and had lots
of meetings and social events. I was picked to go for four days
to Kingston and Queens University to represent our group.
The total cost to me was $12.00. We slept in the dorm and
ate in the cafeteria. It ended with a banquet and a dance. My
first school was the Union School in Goulbourn later being
changed over to Huntley Public School. Around 12-20 kids
in each school with grade 1-8 being taught. My Aunt taught
school for $500/year. I stopped at the end of Grade 8 after
writing my entrance exam at Ashton. My parents could not

afford to send us to high school. By the time I had reached my late teens, my older brothers had gone off the farm to work. My oldest sister was married at 19 years of age. Also, by now my mother was getting more crippled with arthritis and eventually ended up in bed for 12 years before she died. So my sister and I took turns to go out to work while the other stayed home. One sister went to work in the Appleton woollen mill, then after a few years, wartime by now, I went to work for the owners of the mill. I spent over 4 years there. I had my own bedsitting room and bathroom at the end of the house. I cleaned, cooked and washed for $35/month and room and board. I enjoyed my years there and was treated as a member of the family. I attended all the social events in the village hall and church. I had every second weekend off to go home. I remember the day the war ended. Everyone in the village came to the lawn in front of the church and one fellow played the bagpipes. It was such a happy gathering of the people. I then moved to Almonte and went to work in the laundry room of the Almonte Hospital, hanging sheets and baby diapers out on the clothesline but we did have a gas washer and dryer. From there I went to Carleton Place and done housework for $10/week at a Bakery. I did the housework and cleaning there as well as made pies two days a week for the bakery.

A couple of years later I went to work for the part owners of the Findlay foundry. They had a big three storey house with beautiful gardens. While there I married Bob McKenzie after knowing him for over two years. We were married in Ottawa in a United Church minister's home. We went to a photographers afterwards to have our picture taken, then we went to Bob's foster parents for the weekend then back to work

Monday. We lived at my employers for the first winter. Then we got our first apartment for $34/month. I continued to work until my first daughter Nancy was born.

We lived in Appleton for 8 years while the last four children were born. My mother and father lived next door so I helped out there as well as raising my own family. Six months after moving there, my mother died. My father continued to live next door to us for many years. A year in Balderson, and then a move to Richmond for 20 years on Hamilton Street. The kids still think of Richmond as their home. I worked at the Richmond Bakery for 4 years, the Richmond Inn for 8 years, South Carleton High School for 3 years and Richmond Lodge for the first two years it was open. I was always the cook, and that was something I enjoyed.

By now the family are off on their own, but always keep in touch. We didn't have a lot of money when raising our family but with their help we managed and today they make me proud. Our move to a Seniors Apartment building in Stittsville was best for us, as my husband's health declined and it was good to have people nearby. We have been able too to help people who needed help and enjoy all the activities that go on in the building. My family continues to be my greatest support now that my husband has died. The visits, phone calls and outings are all very much appreciated. I in turn try to do my part by being as independent as I can be for as long as I can. I enjoy my church work and my involvement in things in the building. This year I attended the International Plowing match and the Scottish music in Almonte among other things.

I think through my life I have learned you can't run away from the weather, your neighbours, and your problems but try to live each day fully and to do a helpful thing for someone.

In 1996, Janetta was the winner of the 'Blarney' story contest held in conjunction with the upcoming 'Jiggs' dinner being hosted by the Stittsville United Church. The topic of the 'blarney' story was optional but it needed to have an Irish, Newfoundland or Maritime flavour. Grandma drew upon her recollections of many trips to PEI with Grandpa to visit our family in the early 1990s. My grandmother won two tickets to the 'Jiggs Dinner' held in March of that year – I'm sure she likely enjoyed that dinner as much as all the others she had participated in convening over the years during her time in the United Church Womens group in Stittsville, Ontario.

At one of Grandma's birthday parties held at the United Church hall in Stittsville, she had asked that donations be given to the Stittsville Food Bank rather than any gifts for herself and so there was quite a collection of donated food items as well as monetary donations dropped off at the celebration. Janetta was always a giving person. Through her we all learned that to give of our time and friendship was one of the most valued things in life.

When Jennifer, Michael and I were together a few weeks ago, our Mom asked us what our favourite memories of her Mom were; Jennifer comments were – "it is so important to be here right now, Grandma loved us unconditionally. Grandma means pies." Jennifer remembered taking a frozen one home one year to Edmonton and always mittens for the kids; Michael remembered a time when he was a little boy coming from Grade school in Ottawa and Grandma and Grandpa staying with us for a short while – he'd scoot downstairs as soon as he got home, cuddle up on the couch between them both and watch "As the World Turns" before supper; me, I remember the house in Richmond, the dump truck outside and potatoes in the garden; Richmond Fair and Brownie the little dog. There was always pies and homemade buns too! Great Grade 2 memories from my childhood!

Let me now close with another writing by my Grandma, the last remaining of the original Harry Hamilton clan - a little repetitive from the first writing but oh so important to understand who Grandma really was;

Titled Now and Then

As I listen to the television and radio news this past winter and the reports of all the cutbacks in the welfare programs, I am reminded of the time when I was in my early teens – would the young people of today like to live in the thirties? We didn't know any other life and we were happy because everyone was in the same situation. We lived on a farm and there were 7 children in the family. We learned to sew, knit and cook all at home, not in school programs. We learned to bake bread, churn butter, milk cows and take care of sick people at home.

Neither myself, nor my sisters or brothers attended high school. We all worked in a large garden and every summer picked wild blueberries for preserves. We wore simple everyday clothes which my mother had made for us. She would take a man's overcoat and turn it inside out and make a coat for one of us girls. An old piece of fur made the collar. A dress would be remade 2-3 times, a new collar, buttons and belt and it did wonders for our moral.

If a sock had a hole in the heel, the foot was taken off and reknit.

We learned the Ten Commandments, The Lord's Prayer and the 23rd Psalm at an early age.

Birthdays were an occasion. We would put pennies under the birthday person's plate at breakfast time and get them back on our birthday. At supper, a fresh baked cake arrived on the table, with nickels, dimes and quarters wrapped in wax paper in the cake. The older children helped to take care of the younger ones. Babysitters were unheard of. Salt pork was one of or main foods and beef was boiled and the broth put on bread. (to the end, Grandma enjoyed her broth – she kept saying over and over of late that she found that broth so nourishing)

It was a big occasion when the neighbours came to help thresh the grain in the fall and saw wood in the winter. The white linen table cloth was put on the table and the best dishes were brought out. Bathrooms were unheard of and our flush toilets were outhouses. For many families, the Eatons catalogue was the toilet paper of today. Christmas was looked forward to for weeks. If the children misbehaved, they were advised to look under the stove where Santa had dropped a peanut or in some cases a walnut to assure everyone he was watching – (a tradition that carried over to the McKenzie family growing up).

My mother saved Christmas wrapping paper for years. Every Christmas it came out and was pressed with the old black iron heated on the wood stove. Every child received one gift and fruit from Santa.

Mother would warm the handmade quilts around the woodstove before bedtime. We three girls all slept in one bed with a straw mattress. We all went barefoot in the summer and got new shoes for school in the fall.

The Ladies Aid from the church was entertainment for the local ladies where they pieced together quilts for the poor. They also made a quilt with people's names from the church embroidered on it. The people paid 10 cents to have their name on the quilt. Poor as they were they managed to send money overseas to a mission fund.

The papers were not filled with stories of violence but instead local news and helpful hints on how to survive the times. We listened on the radio to war news, Fibber McGee and Molly and Ma Perkins. We were happy and content with the life we had. We knew no other. We helped neighbours who needed a hand cheerfully and with no thought of pay.

No one can change the times or the way each generation lives but there is always hope for a better world, a greater understanding of each other and love for our country and fellow man.

Chapter 4

A New Adventure

After Mom's passing, I seemed to be just existing, not knowing for sure what was keeping me here in this small town? Decision time – looking in the mirror one night before bed, and not liking what I saw, I asked myself, "What's next?" Within a few minutes, no – actually seconds, I had my answer. Back East, I would go. I love the music, the many cultures and the genuine being of the people. I am always drawn to the East Coast, feeling most comfortable there. If I could have the opportunity to live out the rest of my days with the ocean at my door, I would be truly in my happy place. Time will tell.

So, 2018 saw me embark on another adventure. Not knowing what the future would hold, I decided to leave life once again as I knew it and forge a new way forward. Getting in my little blue car and taking off on a 63-day road trip in the spring of 2018 was the most therapeutic thing I could ever have done for myself. I was at a standstill the beginning of the year, immersed in sorrow at the passing of my Mom and, also at the stalling of a friendship that I had thought was much more than that. I had to do something! It was time for something different! So, road trip it was, a little test run to see if I could actually make a bigger change leading to the next adventure, this one for the rest of my life. That road trip gave me hope and a zest for what I was missing in my life. I went back home for the summer months as it was time to gather the kids and their families and have a good old visit and chat, along with letting them in on my future plans. All OK with them!

Finding an apartment to rent in a home in Victoria, Prince Edward Island in the fall of 2018 awakened my heart once again. I make friends easily, always have; no different this time around.

From the moment I arrived at the house in Victoria, I was taken by the eyes that would pierce right through you, of a beautiful chocolate lab puppy, called Clover.

It didn't take long for him and I to bond. You knew you had arrived in Clover's world if he would run at you and go through your legs, "London Bridges" we called it; that and bringing you one of his favourite toys when you came upstairs to the kitchen for breakfast or arriving home at the front door. He always seemed to act the most content when he knew we are all home and accounted for.

I will never forget the lovely welcome dinner the first night I arrived at the house after a long two-day drive from Ottawa, Ontario. The three of us girls enjoying dinner in the sunroom, the dog playing happily nearby. All of a sudden, I felt a swish and away went my cloth napkin from my lap. Apparently this was a favourite trick of this little fella, to get our attention. As the months passed by, I quickly found out napkins were not the only prize, but tea towels hanging in the kitchen were also fair game. He'd run, hoping one of us would try to catch him; great fun.

A chewer though, so shoes and other items of particular interest were locked up out of sight. He still hasn't learned how to open the front closet door, phew!

The companionship this four-legged friend provided was astounding. He was one of us.

Now four years old plus, he has been through so much; elbow dysplasia in his first year and more recently a ligament disease of the knees, comparable to ACL in humans. Coming off the drugs after an operation and, bringing me a stolen napkin was his way of telling me, I'm OK – "it won't be long before I'm back to tricks". Thank goodness, little fella!

Clover has his favourites though I must say – his owner is of course who he knows pays the mortgage. But, then there's that "auntie" who would open the door to come upstairs every morning for breakfast at the Island. The tail started wagging as he sat behind me on the floor watching my every move till I was finished and then it would be time for a cuddle and a lick of the hands, just in case there might be a crumb or two. Every once in a while I received a Clover kiss on the cheek if I asked nicely. But, there's another "auntie" who used to live here before me and whom he loves dearly. When she arrives, we know we are toast. I got that message loud and clear one day when she had just arrived in the front hall and he heard her. I stood in the hallway and called him, just to see what he would do. As I expected, he came running head on down the hall to the front entry, almost knocking me down as he went by to see his old friend. He and I had a chat about that later.

This is my first experience ever with a dog that rings a bell at the back door when he needs to go out. But, wait – somebody rings the bell for attention, too, especially if he's in the dog house! A smart little fella!

As I headed out to share a meal with my old friends here on the Island one Boxing Day, I was reminded of the many lasting friendships we as a family have made over the years as well as the new ones I continued to make as I went about my daily life. I believe human contact is a necessity in each and every one of our lives. We crave acceptance and love, as humans. Where we find it, is mostly up to us.

A tradition always in our house during the Christmas season, when I was just a girl - thank-you notes for those gifts and kindnesses received especially over the holidays and to always take one thing out of the house for one brought in; thus, the bag of hats, mitts, and socks awaiting drop off at the local new to you shop later this week. Thank you Mom for instilling these life long habits in me.

A stack of books sits atop the dresser, a prop used for a photoshoot recently here on the Island. Minimalist that I now am, my actual books kept are few but each of these in the stack have special meaning.

I am humbled - I have been approached by a complete stranger who asked if she could use one of my photos as inspiration for a painting, another writer has reached out to me for advice, a little grandchild recently texted looking for genealogical information for a school project (which of course Grandma had tucked away); "Squiggly" was thrilled at not only the information but the pictures attached. I also continue to be blessed with friends all across this country with whom I can share a Facebook post or an intimate conversation. My life is good, even during this Covid-19 pandemic as I quietly reflect upon years gone by. Deep in thought this morning, I think of all who have crossed my path so far along my life's journey.

There has always been some event to go to with friends or even just on my own – the Clyde River Hall events here on the Island on a Sunday afternoon provided such a reprieve from the long winter days. With a museum downstairs and various speaker series, all left room to the imagination. One particular Sunday afternoon, a speaker described what our ancestors wore featuring a collection of vintage and restored clothing – 2 hours in a packed hall with people from the community and beyond enjoying tea and a light lunch afterwards. Cost – simply a donation at the door to these wonderful winter lectures.

Dinner by oil lamp to plot and plan, the making of another new friendship – awhile back now, but this friendship has again brought the best of things to my heart. This person understands my true love of history and so enlisted me to join her on her quest to keep the history of Victoria, Prince Edward Island alive and well. As most know, I love to dress up and act up, as they say, so I readily agreed to be the schoolteacher of days gone by, at the Heritage Day event celebrated here in Victoria in February, 2019. What fun! And of course, there were more dress up days to come; surprise, surprise!

Every outing was a learning experience – but, most of all, it was the getting to know people in my community, on the South Shore of Prince Edward Island, as well as other locales of this beautiful province. And, especially to reacquaint with those we knew over twenty years ago while here on the Island first with the military, and for the wonderful eight years following.

The provincial election - spring of 2019! History was in the making! What a time I had, from the moment I decided to get involved in the Green Party. Would our efforts be realized on Tuesday night when the polls closed? I was enlightened each and every day of this campaign with the people I met along the way; be it either canvassing with others or assisting in the planning of events. Whatever the outcome of the party then and in future years, I am grateful for the people that crossed my path that spring and of the many friendships made.

Road trips – some appear surprised at how far afield I will go, not me. I am at home in my car and do some of my best thinking when on a drive, be it short or long. Decisions come from these drives, sometimes earthshattering but made with great determination and always rather quickly.

With recent realizations, I now have decided to stay on the Island longer than expected; all part of the adventure! As I am realizing, nothing ever needs to be locked in. One day at a time!

Victoria, Prince Edward Island

Never a day passes that this man is not in my thoughts. Turning the page, realizing I cannot endure the heartache any longer, has been ever so difficult. Try as I may, he continues to tug at my heart, tonight with a subtle Facebook post. It appears his thoughts have taken him in the same old direction again. I feel so sad when I think of how it has encompassed his life for such a long time. It consumes him, heartache consumes me.

I sit up with a start when I see a message pop up on social media – sometimes it's a friend from the old days, or sometimes even from the really old days (my public school days) – imagine! I read the message thinking afterwards how fortunate I am to have someone in my past remember me with such caring words and sincerity. The connectivity of Facebook and other methods of social media, inspire me as well as keep me aware of my family and friends and their activities. It is a quick way to let the world know I'm alive and kicking each morning as my feet hit the floor, as well as show off some pretty impressive photos of my surroundings to those who may not have had the opportunity to have had the luxury of travel to these parts of Canada.

It was late spring of 2019 on the Island and I felt I was on the cusp of something new; I could feel it - change was in the air, as they say. Lo and behold, it was an opportunity that sort of just fell into my lap - tour guiding; I loved it and looked so forward to a few more seasons of this newfound thing called work, but didn't feel like work at all. Walking tours and providing commentary on motorcoach tours opened up my eyes to the wonderful history of this Island and so much more. Unfortunately 2020 was not kind to any of us; however, I am learning to adapt to life with this pandemic. Cruise ship visits to the Island did not exist this year, so I packed up my uniform and materials for another day.

What have I learned most from writing this story (likely things I already knew) - be careful of the word spoken – you cannot take it back. If you are feeling out of sorts or down, look carefully in the mirror. Look at your eyes, they hold the answer. Pick yourself up and go forward on that new adventure, if you don't like what you see. Rid yourself of the energy wasters; think of the last year and your accomplishments, as well as things that just didn't work out. What do you want as your next year? Get out the paper and pen and start mapping out what could be – this is your action plan for tomorrow and every day after. It can change many times in the planning, but oh what fun to plan.

With a goal in mind of providing each of my children and grandchildren a little update on my life travels after the publishing of "60 Odd Years", I have decided to write a short synopsis of each year for the next few – to hand off to them when I am older; my further gift to them, of who I really am. This writing may be in cursive form, short notes to describe the joys of living. I am not sure what the end result will look like but it will be cool, no matter. I love to tell my story!

Now I guess the million dollar question; Love you ask? Did I encounter love as my journey continued? Yes, I did. I will always remember my life with Ray and the love held tight in our hearts for each other those 35 years. We thought we had it all and never dreamt of that coming to a crashing end. As I said earlier, heck, with all the good drugs nowadays, we envisioned living till at least 104. Not to be! So, the answer to the question – yes, the Master had another plan for me indeed. I met someone a number of years later and, found I could actually have feelings for someone else. The purpose of that relationship I'm sure was to have me learn just that, something I never had imagined possible. But then, a few years later, I met someone who I fell deeply in love with. Oh, if only it had been my forever, but no, not meant to be. I continue on now alone, not too concerned about whether that is all there is to love. It may find me again, it may not. In the meantime, I owe it to myself to live again.

May we always be blessed with wonderful memories of those times past but also of the memories we create for ourselves along the way.

Since finishing the actual storyline of 60 Odd Years in the early spring of 2020, shortly after the pandemic had struck, I continue to add footnotes each year following, in order that I remember and reflect.

The year, 2020:

I am grateful for the connectivity of social media, especially Facebook over the years which has kept me alight of the goings on not only in the world, but with my family and friends.

I love to connect with my soul sister in Hackett's Cove, Nova Scotia whenever I can. A trip over to attend a winter party recently reminded me of just why she and I are such friends. Sitting down to watch a serial on TV one evening while there, I was touched at the kindness of her husband wandering off to leave us two together to enjoy the show we both love so much.

Deeply moved over lunch recently with an acquaintance, discussing her childhood and a vivid memory in her life, I was all ears. She would have been likely around 6 years old at the time. Her family welcomed Japanese folks into their home to give them a fresh start here on the Island many, many years ago. She remembered the harsh words against her family by some, but that never discouraged her family or herself in fact. She later went on in life to play a major part in welcoming other families from abroad to our community here on the Island, and has been rewarded time and time again, by the resulting lives of these newcomers to Canada. Well done, lady! I can't begin to understand the comprehension you had as a six-year old, hearing those harsh comments by some, but then seeing that love would indeed prevail.

The things most important to me are family, friends, road trips, writing, taking and sharing photographs, history, libraries and music, in no specific order. These are the things that take up my day and where I find the most enjoyment.

Rattled on many fronts this past year, it is becoming clearer to me as to who I really want to become. It is important not to sell my soul, to write my thoughts down whenever and wherever – such healing powers this process has. This Christmas season, memories of Christmases past kept floating to the surface; then the sadness of a number of people really in dire crisis this past year touched me as well. Eventually one pulls out of this period of "funk". Since Ray's passing in 2006, I seem to have hit ebbs and tides throughout the years, but I always manage to come back to the smiling me eventually, thank goodness. I now know this will be part of my being forever, that love lost and the trauma from its suddenness will stay. I accept that.

And now what would 2020 be without mention of Covid-19; March 2020 and the world as we knew it came to a crashing halt! 03 April 2020 – I have just listened to today's newscast from the Canadian Broadcasting Corporation and our almost daily update from our Prime Minister, The Right Honourable Justin Trudeau, Canada's 23rd Prime Minister. Next up will be the almost daily newscast from Dr. Heather Morrison, Chief Health Officer for Prince Edward Island. These two updates as well as the local news each day provide me with what I need to know; the information all Islanders as well as our fellow Canadians await during these days of holy terror of the Coronavirus commonly known now as COVID-19.

News updates provide new words such as "stark" – the Island here is the most densely populated province in the country, a reminder that we need to all just stay home. Trips out are now limited and for the essentials only. I have even stopped, yes, stopped going for walks even around the village I live in. Hoping we can really flatten the curve as they say, in the next while. We have to give it all we have for each other as well as for ourselves. I must say, though I miss the calming sounds of the waters nearby here in our little village of Victoria-by-the-Sea.

I have so many beautiful photos of Prince Edward Island which I have taken so often on those very outings that I then took for granted. Now, I realize their value as I gaze at pictures of our red coast and the many pictures taken of our beautiful beaches and waters. I long to walk along the beaches, my toes touching where sand and waters meet, with the backdrop of the cliffs of the coast luring me to walk further.

I try to find new ways to entertain myself. I have an apartment to myself in a home here in the village, meeting up with the others in the house at mealtimes around the kitchen island. I am so grateful for my private space, but also for the time spent together buoying each other's spirits. It is so easy to get down with all that seems to worsen each coming day. There is a beautiful chocolate brown Labrador puppy in this house as well who brightens each and every day. He's also missing his trips down to the wharf these days as well. He almost got to the waters on his own yesterday, but you were busted Clover!

I've invented a little game to not only keep in contact with a grandchild several provinces away in Ontario – having trouble with French numbers at school before it closed down so Grandma decided maybe it was time she brushed up on her numbers as well. Ouch! Grandma's French language training was over 50 years ago, but heh, it keeps me and the little one connected when we don't want to spend all our time talking about or thinking about this darn virus thing. I had hoped our planned summer get together this August would happen. There were so many things I wanted to show him, especially cliffs red and looming here along our shore – things I know this child has never seen before. I love the beaches and the seemingly endless walks on the sand and then ever so gingerly I stick my toes first into the water to see how cold it really is. It does take a bit for the water along our coastline to warm up each spring.

To keep myself busy during these days, I reach out to a couple of friends each day, either by phone or email checking to see how things are with them and joking with them about my turning into my Mom, having taken up my knitting needles again. Reading and writing have always been my go-to, so I am glad these are still a couple of favourite past times to get me through these days. No one wants to fall off the cliff, so to speak. I am ever so conscious of my own mental health, more than I have ever been. Not one to get too dragged down by things, even I can reach my point of exhaustion though, so then I realize its lights out for an hour or two. I awaken refreshed and ready to carry on, to be ready after this thing is conquered and enjoy the continuation of the many friendships I am so lucky to have. Once in a while I notice a friend "slipping" it seems, going down the path of no return. Then, I remember we are all in this together, no one wants to see anyone fall off this cliff.

I am more mindful now of things like family, friends (the one I was a little short to the other day), no real schedule in my day – living in the moment now it seems, the only essential trips out likely just for groceries, the re-read of a manuscript I'm ready to send off soon to the publisher and the look back at photos taken over the past year and a half here on the Island, always illuminating the cliffs along the coastline and waters I have so grown to love. I am always, always drawn to the water whether it be a little stream in the woods, waters flowing underneath a bridge, or an inlet, and, always the ocean or the strait nearby.

April 16, 2020 – here we are this morning a couple of weeks further into this self-distancing and it seems to be working; praying that we will indeed flatten the curve in the next little while and be able to have a slow resume to some of our activities, those we used to call normal. Who knows what the new normal will look like, but that's OK – let's put this behind us, learn from it and look forward with great anticipation to a better day.

I must fight the anxiety (the weirdest of dreams taking place some nights as I toss and turn) and depression; it is easy in these times to reach at least in my case for that additional comfort food, perhaps a cookie or an extra treat. Alcohol can also present its own challenges during these times. What once may have been an occasional drink with friends can start to become a little too often. Of that I am conscious and grateful as I've seen the devastation that can bring and I hope never to succumb to that lifestyle. Last evening on the National newscast, I was sobered by the comments from the Premier of Alberta as he spoke about some of the measures they are putting in place for their people – especially the mental health component. Speaking of the likelihood of alcohol becoming a bigger part of people's lives these days, he indicated measures would have to added to assist those then dealing with these unexpected issues once the days of self-distancing and isolation are over.

I think of what I have now done without the last month or so, and if those things were really a priority back then. Shopping for clothing has been put on hold at least till the spring/summer season arrives, only going once a week or so for groceries. Grocery lists continue to change as I think "do I really need that item?" and shortens my time dramatically in the actual store. No more browsing, just list in in hand and, in and out, lickety-split.

I know there is nothing productive to be gained by allowing fear to set in, so I grab that book from the coffee table and take a stab at a chapter or two; all the while calming the mind. It is the mind we can let wander and go places needlessly. Unrelenting times, yes, cause worry – but it's how we react that will make us who we are in the end.

Is this a change in my plan? Fear can set in and stop us in our tracks. Instead, think about life and how precious it is and what it means to you – now and in the future; a time to shed, my priorities are shifting.

I am motivated by my children and their coping skills during this pandemic. They all have their own children and are setting such an example for those kids as to how to deal with this unexpected time in their lives.

I leave you heading into 2021 not with lofty goals, just my goal to further become the person I want to be.

The year, 2021:

My late husband's niece, Jill dies from Covid on January 04, 2021; now we really feel the head on impact of this pandemic. It has hit home. Only 44 she was and now the loss of a whole lifetime that was ahead of her.

The storming of Capital Hill in the United States; Trump is gone; Biden is in!

I was Covid stalled – I had come over to Cape Breton, Nova Scotia last fall to further my adventures in the Maritimes but now stalled again – no movement anywhere due to restrictions placed on us all by Covid. I had been thinking of visiting Newfoundland while out this way but now I am just anxious to get back home to Ontario to see my kids and family there and in Alberta.

Then one February morning up popped a job opportunity but what a hassle to move back to the Island – Covid protocols now in place for entry to PEI? Decision made, it's a 7-week contract with the federal government so will give me something to do until the end of April and then maybe, just maybe I'll be able to finally head for home. I was so fortunate to be able to go back to the house I'd stayed at before and the forever friend there willing to self-isolate with me for two weeks upon my return mid February, following all Covid determined protocols.

I will always remember the great friendships made in the St. Peter's area in Cape Breton as well, while there for that short period. A few rousing games of Phase 10 (a card game new to me) and the occasional outings to Bingo and Armchair Yoga passed the time with friends, although it was so short-lived each week.

The Covid numbers have exploded everywhere, especially in Ontario so now I am stalled once again in my plans to move home - hoping now for end of the summer?

May 21, 2021 – my brother, Kenny dies of heart problems; the first of my siblings gone; again, the pressing need to get home, to be with family.

Finishing my contract with the federal government, I took on a short-term position with Public Health (Province of Prince Edward Island) – screening visitors to the Island at the Confederation Bridge, one of the main points of entry to the Island. The Island is small, densely populated and has only a couple of small hospitals to handle any influx of Covid patients, thus the need for strict protocols at all points of entry either by air or vehicle.

Decision reached – I am going to try to make it home the end of August; God willing.

I took a few days and headed over to Nova Scotia to see my friends there, spread across that province to say good-bye before leaving for Ontario. Not knowing when I'd next be visiting the Maritimes again, it was important to me to see old friends this one last time for awhile.

August 30, 2021 – off we go (myself and a friend from Victoria wanting to come along to visit her son and family too); a great road trip; the anticipation of it all, the excitement – finally we were going to Almonte, Ontario. She would return to the Island after a few weeks visit with her family, but I know how much she enjoyed that trip – a few weeks of a lifetime with her precious wee family.

Once home I started thinking about what was next – I had rented a little granny suite off the side of a friend's house in Almonte, so set about getting unpacked and settled in, not to forget all the paperwork that comes with a move especially between provinces. I noticed a job opportunity working for Elections Canada during the fall federal election, so applied. It was one day of training and then a long day supervising at the polls on the actual day of the election. I would do it again in a heartbeat. It was fun connecting with people, seeing old friends from Almonte come through the hall to vote, just feeling useful. This opportunity further fueled my plans to again look for some part-time opportunities this winter to get out there and keep contributing.

I motor along a more relaxed version of me, now that I am living on my own; Covid has determined a lot of my existence as well as others this past year yet again. I have been spending a lot of my time outdoors this fall, short walks snapping a picture or two along the way which has been absolutely the best tonic ever.

Here it is mid October and I woke up this morning knowing what I wanted to do to further my writing. Finally! I have found true focus again today, plotting and planning for what I want to accomplish with a 'maybe' deadline set for next year – a box set of 5 books all telling my story!

The long grey days of November arrived, a slight smattering of snow on the morning of the 15th; a month which it appears I am not the only one that finds it trying. The greyness of heart and soul is exemplified by what is still going on in the country with Covid numbers and around the world. Restrictions have been relaxed a bit but not enough – anti-vaxxers are still around. The risk of families being broken apart with some getting the vaccine, some not choosing to, remains high. My night dreams have resumed once more – again, Covid related as I learned one of my children and her immediate family had contracted Covid. I am truly grateful that they are on the mend; it seemed a very light dose likely due to being fully vaccinated.

I have found some part time administration work for a non-profit here in town and also some reception work for a retirement home in town, allowing me to get out and engage with people, something very important to me living on my own. I've also been asked to do some volunteer writing for a couple of other groups as well. This will bode me well over the winter with lots to do, filling my days with research and continuing on with these other couple of books I have on the go.

To my children the end of this 2021 year, I say this; I am so proud of each and everyone of you as you show me how you continue to cope through this pandemic and set such an example for your children. I miss you all terribly and can't wait to be together again. Stay safe everyone, continue to wear those masks always keeping just a hint of a smile and optimism underneath.

The year, 2022:

A New Year was upon us; the new mutation of this virus although not seemingly as deadly is here and sticking around; restrictions are now in place once again playing with our everyday lives and indeed our minds; I am grateful a number of my children and grandchildren although being diagnosed with Covid these past few weeks have had mild symptoms, if any and are on the mend.

I continued to work at a couple of part-time jobs; one from home online and the other actually in person. I work in a retirement home 3-4 days a week and find that oh so rewarding – it warms my heart to be able to chat with residents, visitors, co-workers. I have lived on my own for the last number of years and so crave human contact. Most of us are meant to be social beings, myself one of those.

I also continue to write; I take great pleasure in picking up wherever I've left off on an unfinished manuscript and also to research for a couple of volunteer writing positions I have picked up last fall. To see your words on a website with your name attached is almost surreal.

January 29/30, 2022 weekend -what will the next few days or even week bring in Ottawa? The so-called tuckers convoy has wrecked utter havoc upon the city. The number of people, the number of trucks, big rigs and smaller vehicle stalled on Wellington Street and the surrounding greenspace has created a massive gridlock and for what? What started out as a protest planned to emphasize that some truckers are not happy with the current border restrictions insisting vaccines be mandatory for crossing to and from the United States of America has morphed into something way out of control. Rednecks, extremists and the far right and left it seems have joined the cause not for the original cause but to be part of a bigger picture insisting on freedom for all. I noticed a FB post last night that sickened me; a young mother had taken her what appeared to be a 7-8 yr old child to be part of the crowd cheering them on. My mind pondered as to what this young mother was thinking exposing her child to such goings on – especially in the light of the earlier happenings in the day. A dangerous day indeed where there was no respect shown for the tomb of the unknown soldier or the statue of Terry Fox. Stores closed, businesses shuttered, a soup kitchen for the homeless bombarded for what?

I look to this week, and wonder where will this saga of the truckers convoy will end? Our Prime Minister will have to surface at some point; currently he is self -isolating due to one of his children being exposed to the virus. A sobering post yesterday afternoon on FB indicated that he and his young family had been moved to an undisclosed location for their safety. Swastikas on flags, four letter words on flags, signage indicating assassin our Prime Minister loom heavily on all of our minds.

I live about 40 minutes from Ottawa far enough away from the scene but I still feel its impact. I am now advised by public authorities to avoid going to the downtown core or even the city if I can. My rights as a Canadian citizen have been compromised. We live off the main highways that have seen the convoy head to Ottawa so no impact directly to me at that point either. However, what if an emergency vehicle needed to access one of those roadways and could not – the end result would be catastrophic.

I am saddened by posts I see from family and friends indicating they are in support of the protest. I sit and wait for a better day. Are they truly my FB friend or just an acquaintance that I am meeting for the first time? People are troubled, people are divided over whether to get the vaccine or not? I myself have the 2 vaccines plus the booster, my own choice and will get the 4th shot shortly.

Many a sleepless night I have spent since the beginning of this thing. I wonder tonight where we will be in 5 years, 10 years or even 1-2 weeks. Fear robs us of our being and I am determined not to let that happen to me.

Third day in of the protest – it continues to snarl the movement of what we all took for granted in the downtown; the Prime Minister spoke quite eloquently I must say – he will not give in to their so-called demands. He actually announced today that he himself had tested positive for Covid today, and is still isolating with his other family members. It does make one wonder thought how this will all end.

Saddened by comments by some friends on Facebook, I decided early on in the day to unfriend some. Right or wrong, it's the way I have to go about my life. One friend has a lucrative business and yet proud to be in favour it seemed of the tactics of the convoy. I learned yesterday the family was not vaccinated nor would they be. I find that difficult to understand and challenging since when doing business they would certainly have had to come in contact with others, those souls unknowingly exposing themselves to the risk of contracting the disease. Others it seems are full of how they see things done differently and always laying the blame on the doorstep of those currently in power.

Day 6 - It's bad, trucks are still there although their numbers are slightly diminished. The weekend ahead looks intimidating as they have called for a rally Saturday afternoon and there is now word of all hotels in the city being booked solid as well as a Tractor convoy coming from the east end into Ottawa that day as well. Alberta has been the scene of similar protests this week and now it appears Quebec is now on the hit list.

I feel challenged now – it is not safe nor wise of me to venture into the city, and not out onto the highway. You have now affected me! My civil liberties have been threatened. I am sad, I am angry, I am once again stalled it seems in this mess called Covid.

Day 12-13 of the mess in downtown Ottawa; now the Alberta Government along with Saskatchewan has decided to let all go in regard to Covid restrictions? I have family in Alberta and wonder if this is the right move – let me take you back to the summer of 2021 in Alberta where they tried a version of this and look where they ended up rather quickly?

Again, I have spent another night of fitful sleep, if sleep at all; one case in a retirement home I work part time at has now morphed into half a dozen cases or more in a matter of a very few days. I breathe a huge sigh of relief when I rapid test each day before work and the result is still negative.

Thank goodness the outbreak at the retirement home was quickly contained; we now move on with the lessening of provincial government Covid restrictions and await as the rest of the world does to see what this will all mean in the next few months.

The convoy has been dismantled after the invoking of the Emergency Measures Act by the federal government. A couple of key organizers remain in jail, awaiting whatever.

Now, Russia has invaded Ukraine with the likelihood of a war of sorts to follow.

March, 2022 – gas prices are on the rise like never before seen;

A ray of sunshine in my day in early March (my sister-in-law is getting married this summer and she asked if I would coordinate her wedding the day of) – why yes, of course, my friend; I have been so looking for something fun to do; it seems like it's been forever since any of us have had any fun. I pray the upcoming spring does not explode with Covid cases and set us back again – one can only hope we go forward and those that project lifting most of the restrictions is the right thing to do, know what they are doing.

I realized last night I have now been home six months; I can count on one hand the friends I have actually seen in person and spent some time with; Covid seems to have us all fearful of those next steps – when and how do we move forward and try to find some sort of normalcy in our world and beings again? I know my soul is struggling to have that comfort of friends and family back in my real world again – I miss you all so.

So wonderful to have a visit this past week with my grandson visiting his Mom while on March school break from New Brunswick – so grown up now at 14; I am blessed to be able to have adult conversations now with this grandchild and others; recently too, a great conversation with another grandchild turning 21 – talking to her was amazing, just hearing the voice of a now young adult; I can't wait to see this family and others hopefully this summer.

March 11 – another outbreak (Covid) at the retirement home where I work; spreading quickly, but within a short time contained and controlled, thank goodness.

March 21- the day the masks can come off in Ontario, if you wish (still some restrictions in long term care so I will indeed be wearing my mask awhile longer); I stopped in at the grocery store this afternoon and it was really strange to see the cashiers no longer masked; most shoppers still were. The frightening part of this is that this bug is still here – my son-in-laws parents are now both down with Covid.

Mid April – unmasked a lot are, I still wear mine as I feel a responsibility to those I work with and for at the retirement home; my fourth shot coming soon and yes, I will have no hesitation in rolling up my sleeve.

A lull in my writing as cases of Covid are still all around us, yet here we are most unmasked and trying to take back a bit of summer 2022 with some large festivals and events in the works. Will it be OK, who knows, anybody's guess.

July 07, 2022 – cancellation of my sister-in-law's wedding scheduled for end of this month; Covid has hit again; a large number of her partner's family have come down with Covid this past couple of weeks after a small family reunion, so responsibility kicked in – not wishing to lose another soul to Covid, they have decided to cancel the big plans and have a much smaller intimate wedding with a very few present. The realization of the impact sits heavily on me this evening – no need now for the dress bought specifically for this wedding; the fun had shopping for the shoes and purse to match long forgotten tonight. Yes, I will put them away for another day, but again the feeling of Covid's continued destruction is a bit overwhelming to say the least. But, wait – a ray of sunshine emerged the next morning as she invited me to be part of that small intimate gathering the end of this month; Yes indeed, my despair regarding not getting to wear that new dress seems so trivial now; I should have been grateful I had a new dress to put away for another occasion. For just a moment, I had lost total purpose of life.

I leave you with this part view of 2022 as we know it now; may faith, hope and possibility prevail as we move forward through the rest of 2022; without that we are so lost – I look forward to the release of this book and another shortly on my way to that 5 book box set. Writing as always continues to soothe my soul, expecially when I am at my lowest. I struggle with the very strong possibility that my trip to see my children and grandchildren in western Canada may not actually happen this summer. I am possibly only one step away from that trip being cancelled by the airlines due to staffing issues at the airports. If that happens, then a road trip next summer will be a must. Me and my red Toyota Rav 4 – I can see it now; another adventure awaits.

Author's Note

Someone suggested recently I should write a piece about our military life. Such experiences we had from our travels between Ottawa, Ontario > Kapuskasing, Ontario > Petawawa, Ontario > Prince George, British Columbia > Ottawa, Ontario > Calgary, Alberta > Charlottetown, Prince Edward Island > and back to Ottawa, Ontario – where to begin? I remember thinking of our first posting west, and back to the time I had went to the little red schoolhouse and had seen pictures of the Canadian Rockies during geography lessons – now I was actually driving through them and seeing them firsthand; mountain goats on the sides of those mountains remain etched in my mind forever.

"Times were lean those first few years in the military; we managed though. We were blessed over and over so many times with new friends at every posting. Second hand cars, military housing, working hard, having fun and raising our family was the norm."

Acknowledgements

To all of those who have moulded me into the person I have become at 60 odd years of age;

Printed in the United States
by Baker & Taylor Publisher Services